RETIREMENT INCOME LOCK

RETIREMENT INCOME LOCK

How to Lock In Lifetime Income

PAUL PUCKETT

ISBN: 098333532X
ISBN 13: 9780983335320
Library of Congress Control Number: 2015952178
Whole Investor Network, Virginia Beach, VA

I told my daughters they could be anything they wanted to be. They listened and told me that I could be anything I wanted to be. Thank you both!

Oh, if you're reading this, you can be anything you want to be too!

TABLE OF CONTENTS

INTRODUCTION

IF YOU HAVE successfully invested during your working years and have an investment portfolio, congratulations! You prepared for retirement and your financial future is bright. But the investment strategies you used to accumulate wealth must change to meet retirement goals. You will still need growth to keep pace with inflation, but you will now need your money to produce income. It is harder, today, for your investments to generate the income you need during your retirement.

For your parents, income investing was easy. In 1980, income yields on bonds and certificates of deposit were above 10%. Today, CD's are averaging less than 2% and most bond funds have yields below 3%. Producing income is challenging, but the real danger to your portfolio is still on the horizon.

And that danger is in an area of your portfolio that you probably consider the safest investment you own!

Most investors and investment professionals focus on the risks of investing in the stock markets. But the stock markets have always had risks. Most of the risks in the stock markets can be avoided by using a long-term strategic investment approach and by limiting your total exposure to the market. But today, the stock market is not the biggest risk in your portfolio.

The biggest danger facing retired investors is not the stock market!
The biggest danger is the bond market!

Bond prices are primarily driven by changes in interest rates. Over the past 35 years interest rates have fallen and bonds and bond funds have risen in price. In the past, investors not only received bond income but also had capital gains. The future is not as favorable.

The future is likely to be thirty years of rising rates and bond investors could see losses greatly exceeding the low income they are currently receiving. Bonds are no longer safe for investors, particularly those who are drawing income from their portfolio.

Although interest rates change frequently, they generally follow a long-term trend. For over thirty years this trend has been downward and bond investors have benefitted with bonds generating both income and growth.

Remember, in a rising rate environment, bond investors are unlikely to recover their losses for decades!

The purpose of this book is to help you to discover a safer investment approach, the Retirement Income Lock.

RETIREMENT INCOME LOCK

Retirement Income Lock is not a product, it is a strategy specifically designed to produce income that will last the remainder of your lifetime and still provide growth to leave for your heirs.

It combines the time-tested proven investment technique of asset allocation with guaranteed income products that provide protection against rising interest rates.

The process has not changed, but the choice of investments must change to increase income, reduce risks and provide the guarantees you need to enjoy your retirement!

THE RETIREMENT
INCOME CHALLENGE

THE SINGLE BIGGEST financial challenge facing retirees to-day is producing investment income. Interest rates have fallen steadily since the early 1980's. Many retired investors have gradually moved their entire portfolio into income producing investments. Over recent time periods, they seem to have made a sound decision.

But there is a silent income killer creeping up behind income oriented investors - **Inflation**. Inflation reduces spending power. It can be conquered, but it takes time and patience. With retirement often lasting twenty to thirty years or more, investors must dedicate a portion of their portfolio to growth. This means accepting some risks while maintaining overall safety and security.

Retired investors should remember that income invest-ments rarely, if ever, provide the growth needed to beat inflation. The challenge is creating a portfolio designed to provide guaranteed income while maintaining growth with a portion of the portfolio in the markets.

Investors have long understood the importance of asset allocation. They, and their financial professionals, have spread their assets over a traditional asset allocation of stocks, bonds, and cash.

Prior to retirement, the portfolio would be more heavily invested in stocks and as they neared retirement they would shift more to bonds. They rebalanced their investments annually and gained the benefits of a diversified portfolio. At retirement, they would begin receiving social security payments and draw income from their portfolio. Some simply drew the interest and dividends without touching principal.

Others based their withdrawals on the portfolios' total return, a technique known as the 4% rule. The 4% Rule was intended to provide retired investors with predictable and reliable income. During the year of retirement 4% of the portfolio is withdrawn, regardless of the portfolio's income. Over the rest of retirement the original dollar amount is withdrawn plus a little more to offset inflation.

For many years, both methods worked well. But today, neither method is a reliable method for retirees who need safe, predictable, and reliable income. Investors must consider a new method of generating retirement income.

Bond and CD yields have fallen steadily for over thirty years. Investors easily found CD's and bonds with rates above 12% in the early 1980's. Today, ten year bond rates are below 3% and five year CD's often pay less than 1%.

The income produced by dividends on stocks has also fallen. The dividend yield on the S&P 500 was over 5% in the early 1980's. From 1997 through 2008 the dividend on the S&P 500 was below 2% and it is currently estimated to be 1.97%.

In addition, stocks have grown more volatile and investors have lost confidence. In the past decade, investors have endured two bear markets, one beginning in 1999 and ending in early 2003. The other beginning in the fall of 2007 and ending during the first quarter of 2009. These back-to-back losses made it very difficult for investors to remain committed to their investment plans. Many are no longer invested in the markets and missed the market rebound that began in 2009.

Many professionals and investors lost confidence in asset allocation when all asset classes fell during the 2007-2009 bear market. But, asset allocation is a long-term process. Short-term market moves are not relevant over long time periods. The issue with asset allocation is that one of the three traditional asset classes is too risky for investors. Adding additional asset classes while maintaining an asset allocation strategy provides a measure of safety and security far superior to limiting your portfolio to cash, bonds, and stocks.

The concept of asset allocation is actually still the best approach for investors, whether they are seeking income, growth, or a combination of both. But additional asset classes are needed to increase diversification, provide growth, and produce consistent income.

So, what is Asset Allocation?

ASSET ALLOCATION

ASSET ALLOCATION IS simply the process of determining how much of your total portfolio to invest in different types of assets, or asset classes. It is very similar to the old saying, "don't keep all of your eggs in one basket". The three traditional asset classes are Stocks(Equities), Fixed Income(Bonds) and Cash. According to studies, asset allocation continues to be the single most important investment decision you will make. But asset allocation should not be limited to these three traditional asset classes.

Over the long term, asset classes behave differently. Most of the time, particularly over longer time periods, stocks and bonds move in opposite directions. A bad decade in the stock market is often a good decade for bonds. Asset allocation guarantees you will not get the best, or more importantly the worst, investment return for any given time period. By allocating your investments, you decrease the risks of a major loss and increase the odds of maintaining your spending power throughout retirement.

Retired investors need guaranteed income. There is still a need for stocks and cash, but retired investors should also consider products specifically designed to provide guaranteed principal and/or guaranteed income. Adding new asset classes to an existing portfolio provides more diversification and income. It is the only choice when the future is uncertain.

Investors are always in a period of uncertainty. The process of asset allocation prepares your portfolio for the future no matter how any particular asset class performs. A well designed asset allocation is still your single best choice to ensure your spending power lasts as long as you do!

By expanding the asset classes to include investments outside of the stock or bond markets, your retirement portfolio can provide higher income. In addition, the new income may be guaranteed throughout your life.

Asset Allocation is a Long-term Strategy - Think in Decades

When it comes to asset allocation and investing, the key is thinking long-term. Savvy investors think in decades, not days, weeks, months, or quarters. Your investment portfolio should be invested for the long-term. With lifetimes lengthening, you should not assume your money is only needed for five to ten years. Many people are living into their nineties and it is becoming common for people to live beyond 100.

As a result, it is wise for retired investors to invest with the goal of never outliving their income. Fortunately, that is possible today! But, it is not possible to guarantee income for the rest of your life using the traditional asset classes of stocks, bonds, and cash.

TRADITIONAL ASSET ALLOCATION

The table below illustrates the traditional asset allocation approach using the original three asset classes:

Asset Class	Percentage
Cash	10%
Bonds	40%
Stocks/Equities	50%

This asset allocation produced an average yield of almost 11% in 1982. Back then, a retired investor could expect an annual income of $12,000 with an investment of only $85,000.

Today, this allocation produces just over 2% in dividends and interest. As a result, an investor in 2014 would need to invest $600,000 to produce $12,000 of annual income.

And this does not consider the impact of inflation.

INFLATION

Inflation has made it even more difficult to generate an investment income in retirement. Inflation is the rise in prices that actually reduces the value of your money.

The most common measurement of inflation is the Consumer Price Index or CPI.

Since 1980, the CPI has risen an average of 3.27% per year. As a result, it takes almost $3.00 today to have the spending power of $1.00 in 1982.

Remember the sample asset allocation of 50% Stocks, 40% Bonds, 10% Cash produced an average yield of almost 11% in 1982. A retired investor could expect an annual income of $12,000 with an investment of only $85,000.

Today, this allocation produces just over 2% in dividends and interest. As a result, an investor in 2014 would need to invest $600,000 to produce $12,000 of annual income.

When you combine years of steadily falling interest rates with years of inflation, the problem becomes very apparent.

Amount Needed to Produce $12,000 Income

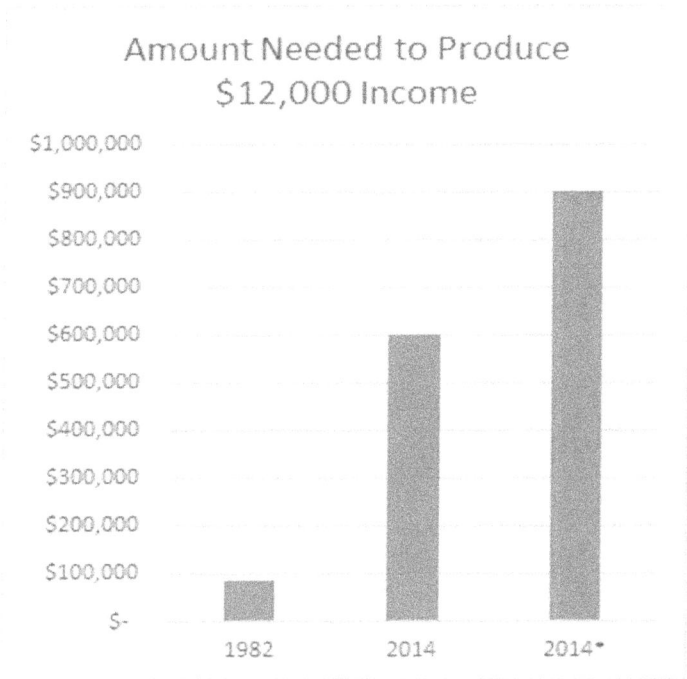

*2014 adjusted for inflation and shows the investment needed to produce $12,000 in 1982 dollars.

To have the spending power of $12,000 annually in 1982, today's retired investor would need over $900,000 in a traditional investment portfolio!

Inflation, combined with historically low rates, has made it very difficult for retired investors to generate the income they need. After spending years preparing for retirement, retirees need to look beyond stocks, bonds, and cash. In the next chapter, we will define the six asset classes retired investors should combine to produce their retirement income portfolio.

Asset Classes for Retired Investors

Traditional investment management has historically depended upon an asset allocation composed of stocks, bonds, and cash. Today, retired investors should include international stocks, real estate, and fixed annuities.

Cash provides liquidity for emergencies and safety of principal.

Bonds have historically provided income, but the risks of loss in the current low interest rate environment may make bonds a poor choice for retired investors.

Fixed annuities provide guaranteed principal and guaranteed income.

Stocks provide long term growth to offset the impact of inflation.

International stocks add diversification and long term growth.

Real estate provides diversification and income.

Each of these asset classes have different characteristics and each has a specific purpose within the retirement income portfolio.

Asset allocation combines the features of each asset class to provide retired investors with growth, safety, and income.

Cash

Definition:
Cash includes checking and savings accounts in banks or credit unions, certificates of deposit, and FDIC insured money market accounts. Cash is the most liquid and accessible retirement income asset class.

Source of return:
Interest paid by the bank or credit union.

Purpose in your retirement portfolio:
Safety, accessibility, emergency fund

Risk:
Inflation

Why invest in cash:
The value is guaranteed and cash is readily accessible when needed.

WHY YOU SHOULD NOT INVEST ALL OF YOUR MONEY IN CASH:
The return on cash deposits is generally low in comparison to other investment classes. Although Cash has the lowest risks of loss of any asset class, more investors have suffered as a result of holding too much in cash than those who invested too much in any other asset class. Investors who have depended on Certificates of Deposit have the same initial investment they originally made years ago. But the long cycle of interest rate changes has put them in a position where the 20% CD bought in 1982, paid 8% in 1989, 4% in 1994, 3% in 2000 and is now earning 1% or less! When inflation is considered, even though they have the exact amount of their original investment, they have lost a tremendous amount of spending power.

THE CASH TRAP
Over short time periods, nothing is as safe as cash. It is perfect for an emergency fund and always available when needed. It is the most used asset class. We use cash to pay for everything whether it is used directly or by check or online. The security of cash is very appealing to all investors. The added protection of FDIC insurance, or NCUSIF for credit unions, makes cash appear to have no risks.

The feeling of safety that comes from having cash causes some investors to hold too much of their assets in cash. They believe cash is safe, and it is safe from loss. But, of all asset classes, cash is the least safe over long time periods. Cash has a low return compared to other asset classes and it is the most affected by inflation. Although the face value of cash does not change, inflation reduces its' spending power. Inflation, as measured by the Consumer Price Index (CPI), has risen an average of 3.27% per year. As a result, a dollar today has the same spending power as thirty-four cents in 1980.

The safety of cash baits the trap that catches many investors. Avoid the cash trap, keep your cash at no more than 20% of your total portfolio and look to other asset classes to maintain your spending power.

Remember, the primary purpose of cash in your portfolio is to provide a source of liquid and easily accessible funds to cover expenses above your income level. Generally, cash should be a minimum of 5% of your portfolio but no more than 20% of your total investments.

BONDS

DEFINITION:
A bond is a loan. When you buy a bond, you are lending your money to a company, government, municipality, agency, or other organization.

SOURCE OF RETURN:
Bonds pay interest and may produce capital gains or losses.

PURPOSE IN YOUR RETIREMENT PORTFOLIO:
Income

RISK:
Default on interest payments or repayment of principal.
Potential losses when sold prior to maturity.
Rising interest rates cause bonds to lose value.

WHY INVEST IN BONDS:
Income from interest payments and potential gains when sold at a higher price.

WHY YOU SHOULD NOT INVEST ALL OF YOUR MONEY IN BONDS:
Risk of loss due to higher interest rates.

HOW TO INVEST:
Bonds can be bought individually but most investors use mutual funds and exchange traded funds to invest in bonds. There is a risk in bond funds because investors cannot hold bonds until maturity when investing in a fund. The fund manager decides when to buy and sell each individual bond based on the objectives of the fund, not your specific objectives.

INTEREST RATES HAVE STEADILY DECLINED
The chart on the next page shows the annual yield on newly issued US Treasuries since 1981. Investors today are

offered very little income in comparison to investors ten, twenty, and thirty years ago.

Note: The US Treasury department did not issue thirty year bonds in 2003, 2004, and 2005. The source for this table is the St. Louis Federal Reserve Bank.

Year	1yr Rate	5yr Rate	10yr Rate	30yr Rate
1981	14.80	14.25	13.92	13.45
1982	12.27	13.01	13.01	12.76
1983	9.58	10.79	11.10	11.18
1984	10.91	12.26	12.46	12.41
1985	8.42	10.12	10.62	10.79
1986	6.45	7.30	7.67	7.78
1987	6.77	7.94	8.39	8.59
1988	7.65	8.48	8.85	8.96
1989	8.53	8.50	8.49	8.45
1990	7.89	8.37	8.55	8.61
1991	5.86	7.37	7.86	8.14
1992		6.19	7.01	7.67
1993	3.43	5.14	5.87	6.59
1994	5.32	6.69	7.09	7.37
1995	5.94	6.38	6.57	6.88
1996	5.52	6.18	6.44	6.71
1997	5.63	6.22	6.35	6.61
1998	5.05	5.15	5.26	5.58
1999	5.08	5.55	5.65	5.87
2000	6.11	6.16	6.03	5.94
2001	3.49	4.56	5.02	5.49
2002	2.00	3.82	4.61	5.43
2003	1.24	2.97	4.01	
2004	1.89	3.43	4.27	
2005	3.62	4.05	4.29	
2006	4.94	4.75	4.80	4.91
2007	4.53	4.43	4.63	4.84
2008	1.83	2.80	3.66	4.28
2009	0.47	2.20	3.26	4.08
2010	0.32	1.93	3.22	4.25
2011	0.18	1.52	2.78	3.91
2012	0.17	0.76	1.80	2.92
2013	0.13	1.17	2.35	3.45
2014	0.12	1.64	2.54	3.34

Interest Rate Risks

When interest rates fall, the value of a bond rises. With interest rates falling over the past thirty years, bonds and bond funds have had better than average historical performance. As a result, many investors have moved a substantial portion of their portfolio to bonds.

If interest rates rise, the value of a bond falls. Interest rates have long cycles that usually last 25-40 years. If history is any indication, investors should be prepared for rates to rise and bond values to fall.

The longer the term of the bond, the more interest rates affect prices. A two year bond will rise and fall substantially less than a ten or twenty year bond. Individual bonds can be held to maturity but, remember, bond funds never mature.

Although bonds have historically been relied upon for their income distributions, today the risk of loss and the low level of interest rates makes bonds a poor choice for retired investors.

The table on the next page shows performance of the Barclays US Aggregate Bond Index beginning in 1981. Price Return does not include interest. Price Return reflects the performance of the market value of the index. Yield indicates the distributions of income as a percentage and Total Return is the combined performance of the principal and the income each year.

PAUL PUCKETT

Year	Price Return	Yield	Total Return
1981	-5.97	12.96	6.25
1982	17.29	13.23	32.62
1983	-3.08	11.74	8.36
1984	2.38	12.49	15.15
1985	9.68	11.43	22.10
1986	5.18	9.64	15.26
1987	-5.99	9.28	2.76
1988	-1.40	9.45	7.89
1989	4.73	9.40	14.53
1990	-0.32	9.30	8.96
1991	6.75	8.85	16.00
1992	-0.18	8.15	7.40
1993	2.93	7.37	9.75
1994	-9.53	7.40	-2.92
1995	10.42	7.37	18.47
1996	-3.24	7.15	3.63
1997	2.46	7.10	9.65
1998	2.04	6.75	8.69
1999	-7.03	6.72	-0.82
2000	4.21	7.04	11.63
2001	1.97	6.58	8.44
2002	4.39	6.13	10.26
2003	-0.43	5.42	4.10
2004	-0.48	5.14	4.34
2005	-2.43	5.07	2.43
2006	-1.02	5.32	4.33
2007	1.42	5.42	6.97
2008	-0.09	5.36	5.24
2009	1.42	4.86	5.93
2010	2.81	4.21	6.54
2011	4.25	3.92	7.84
2012	1.44	3.47	4.21
2013	-4.59	3.23	-2.02
2014	3.01	3.18	5.97

The source for this table is Morningstar Workstation Office edition. The data itself is from Barclays which defines the US Aggregate Bond Index as follows:

"The Barclays US Aggregate Bond Index is a broad-based flagship benchmark that measures the investment grade, US dollar-denominated, fixed-rate taxable bond market. The index includes Treasuries, government-related and corporate securities, MBS (agency fixed-rate and hybrid ARM pass-throughs), ABS and CMBS (agency and non-agency). Provided the necessary inclusion rules are met, US Aggregate-eligible securities also contribute to the multi-currency Global Aggregate Index and the US Universal Index, which includes high yield and emerging markets debt. The US Aggregate Index was created in 1986 with history backfilled to January 1, 1976. "

Since we cannot invest directly in an index, the following table shows a selection of popular, large, bond funds and their performance over the past two years.

Name	2013	2014	12 Mo Yield	Average Eff Duration	Size (Billions)
PIMCO Total Return Instl	-1.92	4.69	4.03	4.87	$ 117
Vanguard Total Bond Market II Idx Inv	-2.26	5.93	2.23	5.63	$ 95
Vanguard Short-Term Investment-Grade Inv	0.97	1.76	1.83	2.41	$ 53
Vanguard Interm-Term Tx-Ex Inv	-1.56	7.25	2.98	4.70	$ 42
JPMorgan Core Bond Select	-1.77	5.21	2.41	4.76	$ 29
T. Rowe Price New Income	-2.26	5.74	2.42	5.32	$ 29
American Funds Bond Fund of Amer A	-1.99	5.53	1.93	5.30	$ 28
Vanguard Total Bond Market Index Inv	-2.26	5.76	2.34	5.62	$ 27
Vanguard GNMA Inv	-2.23	6.65	2.44	4.65	$ 26
Vanguard Inflation-Protected Secs Inv	-8.92	3.83	2.05	7.88	$ 25

When rates rose slightly in 2013, most bond funds lost money. As interest rates fell slightly in 2014, bond funds rose slightly. Surprisingly, the Inflation-Protected bonds had the biggest losses in 2013. Ironically, these bonds are specifically designed to offset the impact of inflation. Many investment professionals recommend these bonds, but their performance has not lived up to expectation.

DURATION

The duration of a fund indicates the anticipated principal loss for each one percentage increase in interest rates. As an example, investors in the Vanguard Total Bond Market II fund receive an income yield of 2.23% with anticipated losses, per percentage increase in interest rates, of 5.63%. Investors face a loss that is more than double the annual income distributed from these funds.

When the interest rate risk of bond funds is considered, particularly given the low yields of these funds, it is clear that investors, particularly those who are retired, should avoid bond funds. There is one type of bond fund that is still appropriate. High-yield bond funds prices are driven more by the economy than by interest rates. When the economy is strong, high-yield bond funds should do well. When the economy is weak, high-yield bond funds fall in value.

Fixed Annuities

Definition:

Annuities represent a contract issued to an investor by an insurance company. Annuities are specifically designed to pay income. For retirees who need current income, an immediate annuity or a fixed annuity with a lifetime income rider can provide current income. Investors planning for retirement may delay their income by purchasing a deferred annuity. For investors who delay income, the interest earned, while the income is deferred, is tax-deferred. Taxes are not due until the income is distributed.

Source of Return:

The return of fixed annuities is income. There is no potential gain or loss as the original investment is guaranteed. All income from any annuity is treated as ordinary income for income tax purposes.

Purpose in your retirement portfolio:

Safety with Guaranteed Income and Principal

Risks:

Most fixed annuities have surrender charges for the first five to 10 years or more. Investors who withdraw more than a specified percentage, generally 10%, in a given year may pay penalties of up to 10% or more of the amount withdrawn.

WHY INVEST IN FIXED ANNUITIES:

Income from annuities is guaranteed, either for a specific period or for your entire life. The value of a fixed annuity is also guaranteed and unaffected by market losses.

WHY YOU SHOULD NOT INVEST EVERYTHING IN FIXED ANNUITIES:

Fixed annuities do not offer the potential growth of stocks or real estate. The actual return is closer to bonds. Like cash, fixed annuities are affected by inflation.

HOW TO INVEST:

Annuities are available through Life Insurance Agents. There are no-load annuities available online, however, these products are not similar to no-load mutual funds and net returns of no-load insurance products may not be higher in comparison to products sold by an agent.

SPECIAL NOTE:

Annuities are complex products and some are not appropriate for retired investors. The NAIC offers an unbiased "Guide to Fixed Annuities" which should be read prior to investing. The guide is free and available from the author or on the NAIC website - www.naic.org. For variable annuities, the SEC provides and introduction at https://www.sec.gov/investor/alerts/ib_var_annuities.pdf. Both are excellent resources for investors considering adding annuities to their retirement portfolio.

FIXED ANNUITIES ARE DESIGNED FOR INCOME, NOT FOR GROWTH! Fixed annuities are designed specifically to produce income. Fixed annuities have set interest rates and guaranteed value. They offer a tremendous advantage to bonds in an increasing interest rate environment because their value does not fall when rates rise.

Fixed Indexed Annuities(FIAs) are a type of fixed annuity that offer interest rates based on various stock market indices like the S&P 500. But, and this is critical, the interest rate is either capped, has a spread, or is lowered by a participation rate below 100%. Many FIAs have both participation rates and caps. As an example, if the FIA has a participation rate of 50% and a cap of 6% and the index has a return of 20%, the interest rate paid by the FIA will be 6%. If the market index falls, no interest is paid and the FIA value does not fall.

The FIA is often oversold by insurance agents who do not understand these products, are not licensed or trained in the investment markets, and believe they offer the "return of the market without the risks".

THERE ARE NO FIA PRODUCTS THAT OFFER THE RETURN OF THE MARKET WITHOUT THE RISKS! While it is certainly true that fixed index annuities offer less risk than the stock market, they do not offer the return of the stock market. Performance of FIAs will be lower than the market when the market rises over the term of the FIA and higher when the market falls over the term of the FIA.

These products are not designed for long-term growth and should rarely exceed 50% of a retirement income portfolio.

Many FIAs now offer Lifetime Income Benefits or Guaranteed Withdrawal Benefits that are an excellent choice for retirees. As an example, an investor in their 60's could purchase this benefit and have a guaranteed income of 5% of the value of the annuity at the time they elect the benefit. So, a $100,000 annuity would pay $5,000 per year for the rest of their life even if the annuity value falls to zero! Many fixed index annuities offer a lifetime payout with an increasing payout. Generally, the payout begins at a lower percentage and increases annually. For investors who believe they may have a long lifespan, it may be appropriate to consider an increasing payout. Payouts are based on your age when you trigger the benefit and typically range from 4.5% for early retirees and 5-7% for retirees above 65.

Keep in mind, the principal of a fixed index annuity is guaranteed against market loss, but income distributions can, and do, come from principal. The rider provides the guarantee that even if you distribute all of the principal through your income distributions, you will receive the same monthly check until you pass away.

Variable Annuities versus Fixed Annuities
Most investors are concerned when any financial professional recommends an annuity. Often, this is a rational concern. Variable annuities have substantial expenses and it is difficult to write-off losses. Most investors are unaware

that there is any difference between variable and fixed annuities, but there are substantial differences. Let's begin with what these two types of annuities have in common.

Any annuity is a contract between an insurance company and the investor. The terms of the annuity contract, or policy, are covered in detail within the policy. All annuities are tax deferred, as long as no withdrawals are made. When any withdrawal is made, the growth or income withdrawn from the annuity is defined as ordinary income for income tax purposes.

Both variable and fixed annuities can be either immediate or deferred. Immediate annuities offer immediate income. The investor writes a check to the insurance company and immediately begins receiving income that is guaranteed for a period chosen by the investor. These choices include:

Period Certain
Lifetime (Sole or Joint)
Lifetime (Sole or Joint)with a Cash Refund
Lifetime (Sole or Joint)with Installment Refund

Recently, insurance companies have begun offering a contingent deferred immediate annuity. Basically, this allows you to purchase an immediate annuity in advance.

Variable Annuities
Variable annuities allow an investor to select from a limited number of sub-accounts invested directly into the market.

A variable annuity will experience the ups and downs of the stock market. There is no principal guarantee.

Variable annuities have several levels of expenses. Some have a charge at purchase, known as a frontend load, others have a backend load, and others are no load. All but the no load variable annuities have a surrender charge that usually last between seven to ten years.

All money within a variable annuity is assessed a Mortality and Expense Risk Fee. According to the Securities and Exchange Commission(SEC)) these fees are typically 1.25%.

Most variable annuities also have "Administrative Expenses" which may be a flat annual fee, usually $25-30, or a percentage, typically around .15%.

Variable annuities also have management fees which vary depending on which sub-accounts are selected. Most variable annuity sub-accounts have management expenses of 1% or more with the money market and bond accounts at a lower level than the equity accounts.

Most variable annuities offer riders which are options the purchaser can add to the annuity at purchase. These riders typically offer an enhanced death benefit, a lifetime withdrawal benefit, or a long-term care rider. Charges for these riders add an additional 1-1.5% in expenses for each rider added to the contract.

When a variable annuity has no riders, the average expense is 2-3%. A fully loaded variable annuities with riders typically averages 3-4.5% annually!

While the concept of tax-deferred growth is certainly valid, the high expenses of variable annuities make them inappropriate for retired investors.

FIXED ANNUITIES AND FIXED INDEX ANNUITIES

Both fixed and fixed index annuities offer guaranteed principal, so the investor is guaranteed against market loss. The guarantee is provided by the insurance company, so it is critical for any investor to choose companies that are financially strong. Insurers are rated by several different companies including AM Best, Moody's, Standard and Poors, Weiss, and The Street.

Most states have State Guaranty Associations that provide investors with limited coverage should an insurance company default. Annuities are regulated by the state and the National Association of Insurance Commissioners, (NAIC), provides information on all aspects of annuity regulation within your state. You can find your states' guarantee fund and what they cover at: http://irionline.org/government-affairs/annuities-regulation-industry-information/insurance-regulation-state-guaranty-associations

The expenses and fees of both fixed and fixed index annuities are not directly stated. For instance, a five year fixed annuity offering a rate of 2.5% would appear to have no fees or expenses. If you invest $100,000 you will receive 2.5% per year and are guaranteed the return of your investment after the surrender charge period, which is generally between five and ten years. But, these products are profitable to the insurance companies, so it is logical to assume the company is making money on your investment. But, in essence, the expenses of these contracts come before the investors stated return.

Fixed index annuity fees are slightly easier to see and come in the form of spreads, participation rates, and caps. Unlike variable annuities, these expenses do not apply to your principal investment. They are assessed only on the growth, or income, of the product. They are designed to limit the investor's growth in exchange for a principal guarantee. As a result, fixed index annuities are not a growth investment.

Many fixed index annuities offer riders for guaranteed lifetime income, long term care, or an enhanced death benefit. Some of these annuities charge fees of .75-1.5% for these riders while other annuities have the charges built into the contract.

Although there are insurance agents who will market index annuities as offering the return of the market without the risk, investors should expect these contracts to offer 3-6% annually over the life of the contract. No fixed index annuity offers the full return of the market.

THE FEDERAL GOVERNMENT RECOMMENDS ANNUITIES FOR RETIREES

Given the tremendous need for security during retirement, the Federal Government has recently recommended annuities to retired people. Their report was released in 2013 and is entitled, Retirement Income - Ensuring Income Throughout Retirement Requires Difficult Choices. The Report focuses on the immediate and contingent deferred immediate annuities, but investors would be wise to consider fixed index annuities with income riders as a more flexible option. The advantage to the fixed index annuity with an income rider is that the investor does not permanently release their investment to the insurance company. To read the report, go to: http://www.gao.gov/new.items/d11400.pdf.

STOCKS

DEFINITION:
Stocks represent ownership. Each share of stock represents a small percentage of the company. These companies can be large, middle, small, or micro sized companies.

SOURCE OF RETURN:
Dividend Income and Capital Gains

PURPOSE IN YOUR RETIREMENT PORTFOLIO:
Diversification and Growth

RISK:
Value of stocks and equity mutual funds fluctuates and your investment has no guarantees.
    You may lose some, or all, of your investment

WHY INVEST IN US STOCKS/EQUITIES:
Over the long-term, stocks offer the highest returns.

WHY YOU SHOULD NOT INVEST ALL OF YOU MONEY IN US STOCKS/EQUITIES:
For retired investors, the fluctuations of the market are too risky. Depending on the sale of stock for income can cause sales to occur when the market is down. US Stocks should not exceed 50% of the retirement income portfolio.

HOW TO INVEST:
Stocks can be bought directly, but investors can eliminate the risk specific to each company by investing in funds. Stocks are available in mutual funds and exchange traded funds. Each fund owns many different companies which provide investors with diversification. Retired investors should have funds that invest in large, mid, small companies in both the US and abroad.

INTERNATIONAL STOCKS

DEFINITION:
International Stocks represent ownership in companies located outside of the United States. Each share of stock represents a small percentage of the company. These companies can be large, middle, small, or micro sized companies.

SOURCE OF RETURN:
Dividend Income and Capital Gains

PURPOSE IN YOUR RETIREMENT PORTFOLIO:
Diversification and Growth

RISKS:
Value of stocks and equity mutual funds fluctuates and your investment has no guarantees.

You may lose some, or all, of your investment

WHY INVEST IN INTERNATIONAL STOCKS/EQUITIES:
Over the long-term, US and International Stocks offer the highest returns.

WHY YOU SHOULD NOT INVEST ALL OF YOU MONEY IN INTERNATIONAL STOCKS/EQUITIES:
For retired investors, the fluctuations of the world stock markets are too risky. Depending on the sale of stock for income can cause sales to occur when the market is down. International Stocks should not exceed 20% of the retirement income portfolio.

HOW TO INVEST:
International stocks have risks but by investing in funds you eliminate the risk specific to each company. Stocks are available in mutual funds and exchange traded funds. Each

fund owns many different companies which provide investors with diversification. Retired investors should have funds that invest in large, mid, small companies in both the US and abroad.

International Stocks add diversification

The US Stock market is now less than 40% of the total stock markets worldwide. Investing internationally offers diversification, which is a critical component of asset allocation. International Stocks represent companies in developed nations. Emerging market stocks represent companies in less developed nations.

Real Estate (REIT's)

Definition:

Residential housing, apartment buildings, retail shops, and commercial buildings are the most common real estate investments.

Source of Return:

Real estate offers income from rent and potential gains or losses when sold. Real estate may also offer tax advantages.

Purpose in your retirement portfolio:

Diversification, Growth, and Income

Risks:
Vacancy can reduce or eliminate income, ongoing costs from property maintenance and property taxes, and potential loss upon sale of property.

Why invest in real estate:
Income from rent, possible income tax advantages, potential gain upon sale of property, and real estate adds diversification to your portfolio.

Why you should not invest everything in Real Estate:
Like stocks, real estate has risks. Retired investors should limit real estate exposure to a maximum of 10% of their portfolio.

How to invest in real estate:
For most investors, REIT mutual and exchange traded funds offer the income and benefits of real estate investing without the direct costs of property maintenance and the time spent in managing the property. REIT funds hold numerous properties and the investor benefits from diversification in property types and location. REIT's must distribute at least 90% of their net income each year.

Real Estate Investing Combines Growth and Income But Not Without Risks
Investing in real estate provides income and diversification, particularly when using a REIT fund. REITs must pay 90% of the income they earn to investors. REITs also offer potential growth, but REITs should be a small part of the

overall retirement income portfolio. Investors should keep REITs at 5-15% of their total portfolio.

THE DOW, S&P 500, AND THE NASDAQ ARE NOT THE ENTIRE STOCK MARKET

If you watch the news, the Dow, S&P 500, and the NASDAQ would seem to be the entire US stock market. But there are more middle and small size companies in the US than those included in these three indices. There are many indices, but also consider the S&P 400(MidCap) and the S&P 600(SmallCap). For the international markets, include both the MSCI EAFE and the MSCI Emerging Markets.

THE MEDIA REPORTS ONLY THE RETURN BASED ON PRICE MOVEMENT

The three major indices reported by TV Stations, Websites, Newspapers, and other media show only the return based on the movement in price. These indices do not show the return including dividends. The table below compares the three US Equity indices showing both the Price Return and the Total Return including dividends.

Name	Ten Year Trailing Return
S&P 500 Price Return	5.77
S&P 500 Total Return	8.01
S&P MidCap 400 Price Return	8.75
S&P MidCap 400 Total Return	10.32
S&P SmallCap 600 Price Return	8.41
S&P SmallCap 600 Total Return	9.68

Although there are numerous investment products that allow you to invest in the stocks that compose an index, you cannot invest directly in the index. The return of stocks is composed of growth and income. As an investor, you will experience gains and losses based on the price movement of your portfolio and you will also receive any income generated by your investments.

The table below shows the total return, including both growth and income, of Large, Mid, Small, International, Emerging Market, and REIT indices 10 year total return, including growth and income, as of March 31, 2014.

Name	Ten Year Trailing Return
S&P 500 Total Return	8.01
S&P MidCap 400 Total Return	10.32
S&P SmallCap 600 Total Return	9.68
MSCI EAFE (International)	4.95
MSCI EM (Emerging Markets)	8.48
S&P United States REIT	9.60

As you can see above, adding investments in more than just the S&P 500 increases diversification and may also increase return. Sometimes the S&P 500 has the highest performance, but often, another index wins.

The Retirement Income Lock portfolio provides exposure to all of the above indices.

RETIREMENT INCOME LOCK

RETIRED INVESTORS NEED a greater level of safety than younger investors. They do not have time to recover from extended market drops. They need their money to generate the income they need to enjoy their retirement. They need an income that is guaranteed to last the rest of their lives.

With lifespans increasing, they also need growth to maintain their spending power. Just one hundred years ago, retiring was a rarity. According to the 2010 US Census, 40.3 million people are 65 or older which is 12 times the percentage of people above the age of 65 in 1900. This number is expected to continue growing. So, retirees need growth and they may need it for twenty or thirty years.

There is no investment, or insurance product, that satisfactorily addresses this combined need for growth and income. Retired investors need a strategy that addresses their needs. This strategy should include investment products, mutual funds and exchange traded funds, that provide long-term growth. It should also include products that offer guaranteed principal and/or guaranteed income.

In the recent past, asset allocation worked but many professionals declared asset allocation "dead" during the simultaneous losses in stocks, bonds, and commodities experienced in the first decade of this century. Asset allocation is absolutely not dead! But, it must be modified to include insurance products.

Asset allocation has worked over the long-term but must be updated given the danger of bond funds in the current interest rate environment. In the past, asset allocation considered stocks as the risky part of the portfolio and bonds were added for safety. In the ideal world, stocks provided the growth needed to maintain, or increase, spending power and bonds provided a level of safety for those times when the stock market fell.

Bonds today do not add safety, they add risks. And for those planning for retirement, and for those living in retirement, these risks are unacceptable. Unfortunately, the problem with bonds, particularly in funds, is not going to disappear anytime soon.

Interest rates typically have very long cycles. The current cycle began in the early eighties when interest rates began falling. They continued to fall for over thirty years. This made bonds the ideal investment for retired investors. In addition to favorable income, bond investors could expect to also have capital gains. Income on bond funds was historically high, with some Treasury Bonds paying double digit income. But today, the risk of loss, when interest rates rise just one percentage point, is often more than double the income generated by these funds.

Retirement IncomeLock combines an investment portfolio with insurance products that offer guaranteed principal and guaranteed income.

Retirement IncomeLock is the strategy needed for those living in retirement. It is much easier for most investors to remain invested during market downturns when they have adequate emergency funds and the knowledge that the majority of their income is guaranteed for life. Retirement IncomeLock allows retired investors to maintain an emergency fund, continue growing their portfolio, and receive a lifetime income.

Recognizing the risk of loss in bond funds, Retirement IncomeLock replaces bonds with fixed and fixed index annuities. For those who have already retired, income riders are chosen that provide a guaranteed level, or increasing, income for life.

Wall Street brokerage firms have attempted to use very expensive and complicated variable annuities to address the needs of retirees. These products are very profitable and the brokerage firms receive annual commissions as long as the investor owns the variable annuity. Variable annuities often offer guaranteed income, but their high expenses make it difficult for them to provide the growth needed to maintain spending power.

Insurance agents focus on the safety of fixed index annuities with income riders. These annuities do provide safety and income. But they are not designed, and should not be expected to provide growth.

It is difficult to find brokerage firms offering fixed annuity products. There are several reasons brokerage firms have resisted offering fixed index annuities. First, brokers offer their clients investment securities such as stocks, bonds, mutual funds, limited partnerships, and variable annuities. Their business is selling investments, but fixed and fixed index annuities are not securities. Because fixed and fixed index annuities have no on-going 12b-1 fees, management fees, or administrative fees, brokers and brokerage firms do not receive annual compensation when they sell fixed or fixed index annuities.

Registered Investment Advisors are fiduciaries, which means they are required to act in their client's best interest. Many advisors do not hold insurance licenses and do not understand the differences between variable, fixed, and fixed index annuities. Investment advisors rarely offer fixed or fixed index annuities.

But, what advisors do understand is that shifting from bonds to annuities represents a substantial pay cut to both themselves and their firm because advisors cannot charge management fees on fixed annuities. If they replace a fifty percent bond allocation with a fifty percent annuity allocation, they take a fifty percent cut in pay!

For most retired investors, it will be necessary to find investment advisors who are also insurance agents to implement the Retirement IncomeLock strategy. This is a fairly unusual combination, but investors could also implement Retirement IncomeLock by using both a broker, or advisor, in conjunction with an insurance agent. Finally, for those comfortable managing their own money, an insurance agent is needed to find a suitable annuity with an income rider.

Today's markets require a combination of investment and insurance products. The next chapter shows the method of building a Retirement IncomeLock portfolio.

RETIREMENT INCOME LOCK PORTFOLIO

B UILDING THE RETIREMENT Income Portfolio is very similar to building a traditional investment portfolio, but there are a few important differences. Let's begin with a review of traditional investment management.

Prior to retirement, an investor focuses on growth and, for income tax purposes, generally avoids any unnecessary taxable income. Asset allocation is a principle of sound investing and, when the objective is growth, the investor allocates their portfolio among three asset classes; Cash, Bonds, and Stocks. Cash provides a source of liquidity and is the best choice for an emergency fund. Bonds add stability and diversification and, in a decreasing interest rate environment, the potential for growth. Stocks provide long-term growth.

ASSET ALLOCATION WITH CASH, BONDS, AND STOCKS

Asset Class	Percentage
Cash	10%
Bonds	40%
Stocks/Equities	50%

This asset allocation was designed for a retired investor seeking income with growth to maintain spending power. It is limited to Cash, Bonds, and Stocks. In the current investing environment, this portfolio has higher risks than in the past. As discussed in an earlier chapter, the stock market has not changed but, today, the bond market has substantial investment risks and produces very low income.

The Retirement Income Portfolio is designed to provide retirees with higher and safer income, long-term growth to maintain spending power, and reduce investment risks.

Asset Class	Percentage
Cash	10%
Bonds	0%
Fixed Index Annuities	50%
Stocks	40%

By replacing bonds with fixed annuities and adding international stocks and real estate, today's retired investors can enjoy their retirement without worrying about their income or their investments.

The Traditional Asset Allocation portfolio income is based on current interest rates and dividends as of September 2014. The Retirement Income Portfolio income is based on dividends and average guaranteed lifetime annuity income payments for a 65 year old retired investor. Income generated by the Retirement Income Portfolio is partially based on the age of the investor. The Retirement Income Portfolio would have higher distributions for older retired investors. For retired couples with a joint income payment, the Retirement Income Portfolio would have slightly lower income than illustrated.

Safety Comparison

Asset Class	Traditional Allocation	Retirement Income	Guaranteed
Cash	5%	10%	Yes
Bonds	55%	0%	No
Fixed Annuities	0%	40%	Yes
US Stocks	45%	35%	No
Int'l Stocks	0%	10%	No
REITs	0%	5%	No
Total Guaranteed	5%	50%	

By eliminating bonds from the Retirement Income Portfolio, the guaranteed portion of the portfolio increases from 5% of the portfolio to 55%! In addition, the majority of the income is now guaranteed! Please note, fixed index annuities are guaranteed by the issuing company.

THE RETIREMENT INCOME PORTFOLIO

The Retirement Income Portfolio is designed for to-day's retired investor. It eliminates the risks of holding bonds and bond funds in a low interest rate environment and provides a higher level of income than a traditional portfolio.

The table below illustrates the increase in income gener-ated by the Retirement Income Portfolio compared to the Traditional Asset Allocation portfolio based on a 65 year old retiree.

Portfolio Size	Traditional Portfolio Annual Income	Retirement Portfolio Annual Income	Difference
$100,000	$4,000	$6,000	+$2,000
$250,000	$10,000	$15,000	+$5,000
$500,000	$20,000	$30,000	+$10,000
$1,000,000	$40,000	$60,000	+$20,000

Conclusion

I T IS NOT difficult to build a safer more reliable investment portfolio that will fund your retirement for your lifetime. Many investors may choose to handle the investment portion of the portfolio on their own using no-load funds or exchange traded funds held at a discount brokerage firm. This can be a valid choice, but isn't retirement about your life, not your money?

In over two decades of working with retired investors, it has been my experience that the happiest retirees have spent the majority of their investment time choosing an advisor. They monitor their advisor which requires less time than monitoring the markets. They are free to live their lives without the daily monitoring of the markets and they avoid the stress that comes from daily market moves.

Remember that money is not your life, or at least it shouldn't be. Your time is infinitely more valuable than your money. Plan accordingly.

ABOUT THE AUTHOR

A FINANCIAL SERVICES PROFESSIONAL since 1988, Paul has extensive experience working primarily with retirees and investors who are planning for retirement. He began his career as a life insurance agent and has served as a loan officer, trust officer, registered representative, investment advisor and private client advisor with several major banks. He is an experienced estate planner who settled over 160 estates.

Over the past 27 years, he has experienced the highs and lows of the markets and strongly believes investors benefit from a long-term, strategic, approach. He manages money based on the time tested technique of asset allocation based on modern portfolio theory. He believes retirement income should be safe and guaranteed, but also recognizes that all investors should maintain growth within their portfolio. For retired clients, he combines traditional equity investing with fixed annuities to help clients have guaranteed income, beat inflation, maintain their spending power, and leave a legacy to their heirs.

Paul is an investment advisor representative and insurance agent serving clients in Virginia and Florida and is the author of <u>Investiphobia: Overcome Your Deepest Investment Fears</u>.

For More Information

I F YOU ARE a resident of Florida or Virginia, I am available to answer any questions you may have on the Retirement Income Portfolio, Investing, Annuities, Life Insurance, Estate Planning, or Long-term Care Insurance.

Please email me at paul@retirementincomelock.com or call me at 757-403-0707 or 941-275-4556.

Disclosures

Paul Puckett is the author of this eBook, Retirement Income: How to Manage Your Money in Retirement. He is also the author of Investiphobia: Overcome Your Deepest Investment Fears. Both books are available on Amazon.

Paul is an investment advisor representative of Q1 Advisors in Virginia Beach and an independent life insurance agent. When retained to manage money, Paul is a fiduciary. This means he is required to put his client's interest first. When working as an insurance agent, he is required to adhere to all insurance regulations and make sure that any product purchased through him is suitable to the investor.

Paul does not offer tax preparation, tax advice ot legal advice. He believes that retired investors should have a team composed of an attorney, accountant, and a financial professional.

This book is intended to provide general investment information for retired investors.

www.ingramcontent.com/pod-product-compliance
Lightning Source LLC
Chambersburg PA
CBHW032307210326
41520CB00047B/2268